THE LAST BOOKS OF HÉCTOR VIEL TEMPERLEY

THE LAST BOOKS OF HÉCTOR VIEL TEMPERLEY

TRANSLATED BY STUART KRIMKO

Published within the framework of Programa SUR
Translation Support Program of the Ministry of Foreign Affairs
International Trade and Worship of the Argentine Republic

SAND PAPER PRESS
KEY WEST

THE LAST BOOKS OF HÉCTOR VIEL TEMPERLEY
Copyright © 2011 The Estate of Héctor Viel Temperley
Translation copyright © 2011 Stuart Krimko
Interview copyright © 1987 Sergio Bizzio
All rights reserved

This edition contains English translations of Héctor Viel Temperley's *Crawl* (1982) and *Hospital Británico* (1986), originally published in Buenos Aires, Argentina, by Par-Avi-Cygno. They were also published in *Obra Completa* (2003) by Ediciones del Dock, Buenos Aires. Sergio Bizzio's "Viel Temperley: State of Communion" originally appeared in *Revista Vuelta Sudamericana*, No. 12, Buenos Aires, 1987.

Cover image: Héctor Viel Temperley with his daughters Veronica and Clara.
Photo by Maruca Viel Temperley, 1965.

This book was designed for Sand Paper Press by David Janik.
The text is set in Sabon. Title pages are set in Grotesque.

Library of Congress Control Number: 2011939293

ISBN 978-0-9843312-4-6

SAND PAPER PRESS
716 LOVE LANE
KEY WEST
FLORIDA
33040
USA

http://sandpaperpress.net

CONTENTS

Introduction vii

Crawl...1

Hospital Británico 55

Viel Temperley: State of Communion
(Sergio Bizzio, 1987) 89

Acknowledgments 95

INTRODUCTION

Héctor Viel Temperley was born in Buenos Aires in 1933. He died there, from cancer, in 1987. At the time of his death he was known among a small group of Argentine writers for the surreal, mystical poetry he had been writing and publishing since he was 23. His last two books in particular, *Crawl* (1982) and *Hospital Británico* (1986), were regarded for their radical formal structures and spiritual intensity. These are the works that appear in this volume, translated into English for the first time.

Little information about Viel Temperley's life exists in the public record. Born into a prominent Buenos Aires family, he achieved early literary success with his 1956 book *Poems with Horses*, which won a prize from the Argentine Society of Writers. *The Swimmer*, his second book, was brought out by Emecé, the major house that published Jorge Luis Borges. He worked first as a journalist, and later as the director of his own advertising agency. He was married and fathered seven children, but lived an increasingly solitary life dedicated to spiritual contemplation and the writing of poetry. His later books were all published by small, independent presses; many of them were difficult to find until Ediciones del Dock published his collected works, posthumously, in 2003. Mostly he shunned literary society, though he did have a few prominent fans, including the wide-ranging writer and cultural figure Fogwill. He preferred the company of the Benedictine monks whom he visited periodically at the monastery in Los Toldos, a small city 200 miles west of Buenos Aires perhaps best known as the birthplace of Eva Perón.

A rare window into the poet's life can be found in his daughter Soledad Viel Temperley's autobiographical novel *Like Arrows in the Hand of a Warrior* (Imprenta Cáritas, 2000), which includes excerpts from letters he sent her in 1984. "I don't belong to society," he wrote on May 22 of that year, "or at least I dream about not belonging to it, and so I live neither well nor badly but with the belief that such superficial pride helps me focus my energies inward as I search for an escape to another world." By this time he had stopped working at the advertising agency and was occupying a spartan Buenos Aires apartment without most of the trappings of modern life. Soledad describes him as living "more and more like a prayer... without a telephone, a radio, or a television, but with reams of blank paper, a cross... a thick dictionary, and the Bible."

Especially in his later books, Viel Temperley's spirituality was the engine for highly innovative, even idiosyncratic, poetic forms. He nonetheless insisted that he not be called a religious writer. "I might be a mystic, a surrealist poet, whatever you want, but not religious. I write about sailors and swimmers," he famously remarked in an interview with the writer and filmmaker Sergio Bizzio conducted just before he died. (The full interview is included at the end of this volume.) A reader familiar with his work would be forgiven for thinking that Viel Temperley was playing the contrarian, but perhaps he was pointing out, correctly, that his poems have little to do with what is commonly referred to as religious literature. He was concerned with dream-like figures, narrative contradictions, and even, on occasion, sexual imagery, all hallmarks of a classically avant-garde artistic practice. Even when he did address spiritual themes head-on, his approach contained more than a hint of erotic tangibility: "I don't orient myself towards [Jesus Christ] by putting aside my love for the girl lying next to the lamp: I look for him there," he told Bizzio, just after admitting that religious pursuit was the driving force behind the composition of *Crawl*:

I had the opportunity to just forget about everything, I shut myself in with a title, *Crawl*, and the intention to give testimony of my faith in Christ, whom I had never named before: I said "God"; a pantheistic god, not the son, the man... I ended up explaining how to swim, how to position the hands when swimming... But I discovered that in order to write *Crawl* I had to learn to pray, and I began to have a distinctly new relationship to prayer and the breath... And at the end of the day I found that I was mentioning him as "this man" or "that man," with lower case letters, because in that moment of my spiritual life it would have been a lie to repeatedly put down "Jesus Christ." Throughout the entire book I only call him by name a single time... I gave testimony. Big deal.

For the poet of *Crawl*, a relationship with Christ comes down to a question of vocabulary. Also important is the connection between the divine and the breath, our primary model for rhythm and repetition. Each of the book's sections begins with an identical refrain, "I come straight from communion and I'm in ecstasy," which goes on to engender chains of images and associations that whisk the reader through beach landscapes, Biblical references, and haunting vignettes (including a scene in which a young dock hand and his bride embrace before she "sells her body / to guests"). Structurally, the ecstatic revelation gives rise not to a definitive version of mystical experience, but an ever-changing one that cannot be contained by linear narrative progression nor easy moral codes. Rising to the self-appointed challenge of uttering Christ's proper name is no "big deal" when seen in the larger context of tropes the poem establishes. More important is the movement from one trope to the next, and the willingness to leave testimony behind as soon as it is given. The arrangement of the poem on the page has a special relevance that furthers this idea:

If you look at *Crawl* from above it moves like a swimming body. I spread the poem out on the floor and stood on a chair to see if there were things that exceeded the pattern. I spent hours above that chair smoking and

looking, and making corrections so that it would have that form... I
wanted it to be like breathing, I wanted each stroke to represent a breath.

Soon the breath would take on new, ominous significance. Viel Temperley
had always been an avid swimmer, and photographs show a strapping
man who took pride in his vigor. In her novel, Soledad describes her father
as a man who lives "life without resting, as fully as humanly possible,"
who shows "impressive discipline when it comes to writing, exercising,
chopping wood, swimming, and praying. Death," she was certain, "will
find him as he's doing the Crawl, his favorite stroke." As early as 1984,
however, he wrote Soledad that he was having difficulty breathing.

What began as a cancer of the lung was not easily contained. Less than
two years later he was admitted to the British Hospital in Buenos Aires for
surgery to remove a tumor from his brain. Fate would have it that his
mother was dying in another hospital nearby. After the operation, in an
understandably impressionable state, Viel Temperley began his
convalescence by experiencing "a feeling of love so intense that it ruined
worldly life." He returned home and tried to maintain this intensity by
writing, and, perhaps even more importantly, reading and reassessing his
previous poetry; the results of these activities resulted in a series of prose
poems that would become *Hospital Británico*, his final work.

The book begins with a short poem, "Hospital Británico: Month of
March, 1986," in which the poet , his head bandaged, is visited in heaven
by his mother. Meanwhile, twenty blocks away, "she lies dying." From the
beginning it's unclear whether these scenes take place on Earth or beyond
it. All we know is that this Rosetto Pavilion in which the poet convalesces,
like a "long corner of summer" or an "armor of butterflies," is no ordinary
hospital wing. Upon turning the page, the reader also quickly discovers
that this is no ordinary volume of poems. A second iteration of the
opening poem awaits, its title slightly amended: "Hospital Británico:
Month of March, 1986 (Version with splinters and 'Christus Pantokrator')."
The "splinters" are in fact phrases from the original poem that are

repurposed as headings for clusters of short texts that follow. Most of these are dated, though some are not. In a note at the end of the book, Viel Temperley reveals that the former were taken from earlier poems, and that the dates indicate the publication dates of the books in which they originally appeared. (Even readers who are encountering his work for the first time here will recognize passages drawn directly from *Crawl*, their line breaks removed and images recontextualized.) The undated passages, meanwhile, are identified as those that were written in March of 1986, after he had undergone the procedure that would leave him with what he described to Bizzio as "a hole in his head." He went on to explain:

> The man who wrote that poem doesn't exist anymore... I gave it an order, I wrote the parts about my mother's death... and the rest was done by a guy who was in a state of having left reality... Who the hell put that thing together? I have no idea. I'm not the author of *Hospital Británico* like I was the author of *Crawl*. *Hospital Británico* is something that was in the air. I did nothing more than find it. *Hospital Británico* allows me to believe that I left the world and I don't know what for. Heaven was in the nurse passing by.

The "splinters" allowed Viel Temperley to create a place where the past and the present could coexist, and latent connections between them could rise to the surface. He even identified early harbingers of his illness: under the title "**My head is bandaged** (distant prophetic text)" is a fragment from 1978 that reads, "My head passes through the fire of the world to be born but keeps a winding stream of frozen water in its memory. And I ask it to help me." Having "left reality," he was able to see his life's work anew, and from a perspective that bordered on omniscience.

The inclusion, then, of Christus Pantokrator among the boxers, dwarves, and harpooners that populate *Hospital Británico* is telling. This imposing icon, often found rendered in mosaic high in the semi-domes of Byzantine churches, stares knowingly at a world balanced between the mortal and the divine. In many cases the two sides of his face feature two different expressions, one skeptical and the other serene, evidence that Christ was miraculous because he represented both God and man. Can anyone say for sure which side stands for which? Like the "something in the air" that inspired Viel Temperley to dramatically reassess his own poetry, the visage of the Pantokrator became a place of faith and inquiry, a zone where he could "dig into the perspiration of all [his] summers," despite the fact that death was upon him. Perhaps it is no coincidence that this passage, the only one dated "Month of April, 1986," was the last in the book to be written. Bathed in memory and sweat, Viel Temperley was discovering that elegy gives rise to ecstasy, and that life is a fever dream built from facts.

S.K.

CRAWL

Pondré su mano sobre el mar

Salmo 89,26

J'attends les cosaques et le Saint-Esprit

Léon Bloy

I will set his hand over the sea

Psalm 89,25

J'attends les cosaques et le Saint-Esprit

Léon Bloy

EL ESPIGÓN MÁS LARGO, EL AVISO
Y EL CRAWL

THE LONGEST JETTY, THE ADVERTISEMENT
AND THE CRAWL

Vengo de comulgar y estoy en éxtasis,
                    aunque comulgué como un ahogado,

mientras en una celda
                    de mi memoria arrecia
                    la lluvia del sudeste,

                              igual que siempre

embiste al sesgo a un espigón muy largo,

                    y barre el largo aviso
                    de vermut que lo escuda

                    con su llamado azul,
                    casi gris en el límite,

I come straight from communion and I'm in ecstasy,
                though I took it like a drowned man,

while in a cell
                of my memory the rain
                from the southeast intensifies,

                                and like always

it mounts a slanting attack on a very long jetty,

                and sweeps across the long vermouth
                advertisement that shields it

                with its blue call,
                almost gray at the edge,

para escurrirse por la tez del mundo
            hacia los ojos de los nadadores:

            dos o tres guardavidas,
            dos adolescentes

y un vago de la arena que cortaron
            con una diagonal

            el mar desde su playa.

To drain through the face of the world
                toward the eyes of the swimmers:

                two or three lifeguards,
                two teenagers

and a wanderer of the sands who cut
                along a diagonal

                      the sea from its beach.

Vengo de comulgar y estoy en éxtasis
junto al hombro del kavanagh y de cara

a la escuela de náutica
y al plátano,

hacedores de fuego que me impiden
flotar con éste entre esos pocos hombres

que allá —solos y lejos con la punta
del espigón desierto—,

mecidos como sábanas

y cobijando, ingrávidos,
la vida en ese extremo

de monedero roto,
de chubasco enfrentado,

10

        I come straight from communion and I'm in ecstasy,
by the shoulder of the kavanagh and face

            to face with the sailing school
            and the plane tree,

            creators of fire that won't let me
float with this man apart from the few

            over there —far off and alone by the end
                    of the deserted jetty—,

            shaken like sheets

                and sheltering, weightless,
                life at that terminus

                of torn change purse,
                of squall met head-on,

desasidos de todo
piensan en el regreso:

descansan; se dan vuelta —en silencio—, y se tienden

otra vez boca abajo,

con un brazo apagando los graznidos
de las gaviotas

y las alas.

freed from any
thought of turning back:

they rest; they turn around —silent—, and stretch out

      face down again,

      waving an arm to extinguish the cries
      of the seagulls

      and their wings.

Vengo de comulgar y estoy en éxtasis
                    contemplando unas sábanas
                    que sólo de mí penden

                    sin querer olvidar que en esta balsa,
de tiempo que detengo y de escafandra

                              con pasos de mujer,
                              nunca fui absuelto

            en el adolescente y en el viento

ni en la cuerda del crawl, que de los hierros
                    cavernosos comienza
                    a separarse;

ni siquiera en las manos deslizándose

I come straight from communion and I'm in ecstasy
                    staring at sheets
                    draped from my body alone

                    not wanting to forget that on this raft,
of time that I stop and of wetsuit

                              with a woman's steps,
                              I was never absolved

                    in the teenager and in the wind

nor in the thread of the crawl, which from its cavernous
                    leg irons begins
                    to escape;

not even in my hands gliding gently

ni en el agua —que corre entre los dedos—

ni en los dedos, ligándose despacio

para remar con aprensión
de nuevo

allí donde no hay mesa para apoyar los brazos

y esperar que alguien venga
desde su pueblo a visitarnos;

nadie fuma ni duerme, y —en días
de gran calma—

sobre el plato de un hombro

puede viajar un vaso.

nor in the water —which runs through my fingers—

nor in my fingers, slowly coming together

        to paddle with apprehension
        once more

in a place where there's no table to rest our arms

        and wait for someone to come
        from their hometown to visit us;

nobody smokes or sleeps, and —on days
                of dead calm—

        atop the plate of a shoulder

        a glass can ride.

Vengo de comulgar y estoy en éxtasis
y no me está mareando un sexo, una fisura,

sino una zona:

el patio de esa escuela
de náutica sin velas —¡cuerpo solo!—

donde unos niños ciegos,
envueltos en miocardio,

con tambores y flautas
reciben a las costas;

la carne comentando,
ya hasta en la espalda,
el frío

—que asciende repentino donde parte el océano

I come straight from communion and I'm in ecstasy,
and what's making me nauseous isn't a sex organ, a crack,

but an area:

the patio of that sailing
school without sails —a body alone!—

where blind kids,
swathed in myocardium,

bang drums and play flutes
to welcome the coasts;

the flesh philosophizing,
even up the back,
the chill

—that abruptly ascends where the ocean parts

y las yemas, heladas,
en su Pudor se pierden—;

y el miedo que, en el vientre, de su piel hace párpado

—entre el ojo que tiembla
y el ojo del abismo—,

y es cordel, por el pecho, de la voz que naufraga

en el aire que hierve, despedido
como sangre,

en los pómulos tronantes.

Peces de cima,

cajas bamboleadas.

and fingertips, frozen,
disappear in its modesty—;

and the fear that, in the belly, makes of its skin an eyelid

—between the eye that trembles
and the eye of the abyss—,

and is a line, through the chest, from the voice that sinks

in the boiling air, shed
like blood,

into thundering cheekbones.

Fish on high,

swinging crates.

LAS ARENERAS, JESUCRISTO
Y EL DESAGÜE

THE SAND QUARRIES, JESUS CHRIST
AND THE SEWER

Vengo de comulgar y estoy en éxtasis
                    aunque comulgué con los cosacos
sentados a una mesa bajo el cielo

                    y los eucaliptus que con ellos
se cimbran estos días bochornosos

                    en que camino hasta las areneras
del sur de la ciudad
                    —el vizcaíno,
                    santa adela,
                    la elisa—

(a la sombra hay un loco, y hay un árbol

                    muy alto

            y alguien dice "cristo en rusia")

I come straight from communion and I'm in ecstasy
                    though I took it with the Cossacks
seated at a table beneath the sky

                    and the eucalyptus trees that sway
alongside them these muggy days

                    when I walk to the sand quarries
south of the city
                    —el vizcaíno,
                      santa adela,
                      la elisa—

(there's a lunatic in the shade, and a very tall

                                tree

            and someone says "christ in russia")

e insolado hablo al yo que está en su orilla,

ansío su aventura
en otro hombre,

y a la hora en que no sé si tuve esclava,
si busco a dios,
si quiero ser o serme,

si fui vendido a tierra o si amo poco,

sé que Él quiere venir pero no puede
cruzar —si no lo robo como a un banco
pesado de galeote—
esa balanza

que es tanta hacia ambos lados
atrancando mis puertas:

la abierta, marginal, no interrumpida
matriz sin cabecera
donde gateó la vida,

donde algunos gatean

y su alma sólo traga lo mismo que el mar traga:

aletas, playas solas e iguales, hombres débiles

y una pared espesa
de cetáceo y de fábrica.

26

and sunstricken I speak to the self on its shore,

        I yearn for its adventure
        in another man,

and in the hour of not knowing if I've kept a slave,
        if I look for god,
        if I want to be or be myself,

if I was sold to earth or if I love a little,

        I know He wants to come but can't get
across —unless I steal him as if from a bench
        heavy with galley slaves—
                that balance

so equally weighted toward both sides
        barring my doors:

the open, liminal, continuous
        womb without source
        where life creeped in,

            where people creep in

and its soul only swallows what the sea swallows:

flippers, beaches lonely and identical, weak men

        and a thick wall
            of cetacean and factory.

Vengo de comulgar y estoy en éxtasis
—De los labios colgado, o de la hostia—,

       hospital retraído respirando;

Y, sangre en celosía, en ella dejo
         pulsos, piel, carcajadas de cosacos
Que de mohamed no aceptan ser vasallos,

      hasta besarme el Rostro en Jesucristo

Detrás de los cabellos del vago de la arena,
       donde los confesores no caminan,

En mi conciencia,   que tragué —sacrílego—

        con Él,   que ve el limón,
            la cal, el sexo

                    I come straight from communion and I'm in ecstasy
—Hanging from my lips, or from the host—,

            a reclusive hospital breathing;

And, in blood like latticework, I leave
                    pulses, skin, cackling of Cossacks
Who won't admit they're vassals of mohammed,

            until I kiss my very Face in Jesus Christ

Behind the tresses of the wanderer of the sands,
                    where confessors don't step foot,

In my conscience,   which I swallowed —sacrilegious—

                    with Him,   who sees lemon,
                            whitewash, sex,

—La puerta azul de gasa tijereteada, huraña,
              de la casi casilla
                          que la belleza puso

En las costas del yo, que en sus muros enyesa

                las huellas de gaviotas
                    de unas cuantas palmeras—

Y el ropero en la torre, el revoltijo de disfraces
                      ácidos contra el pubis,
                  no en las perchas,

                que fue el amor tardío,

                de un cajón de la tierra

Ya en Él, que hace mi ahora entre costillas
                —como vendas de espacios sin memoria—

Dentro del caracol que usé de pecho
                al lado de un diluvio,
                      en una mesa

De plana luz de Cuerpo descendido
                y pétalos volando como llagas,

—The blue door of snipped gauze, turned inward,
                    to the half-built hut
                              beauty put up

On the shores of the self, where the footprints of seagulls

                    from a few palm trees
                         are plastered to the walls—

And the wardrobe in the tower, the pile of acidic
                              costumes against the pubis,
                                   fallen from their hangers,

                    that was belated love,

          from a box in the ground

Already within Him, who makes my now between ribs
                    —like bandages on spaces without memory—

In the shell I used as a breast
                    beside a flood,
                                   on a table

Of flat light from Body descended
                    and petals flying like wounds,

31

O en esa estrecha pieza,   con un sapo,

                    donde brama el motor
                    y no entra el viento

Y a ojos bajos, garganta con naranjas,

                    treguas de voz,

                    se acercan los caballos.

Or in that narrow room,   with a toad,

> where the engine roars
> and the wind stays out

And with lowered eyes, a throat with oranges,

> halting speech,

> the horses approach.

Vengo de comulgar y estoy en éxtasis
Y hacia otro hombre apuntan los prismáticos

De la escuela de náutica   —que resistí— y del plátano

Que no sé más cuál es,   que está en el puerto
                    con otros cien,

                                   que un día fue ciruelo

O grito de novicia de piletas vacías
                    rotas por el allá,
                                   después zureo

De torcaza escondida en los portones
                    calientes de un estadio en el suburbio

                    I come straight from communion and I'm in ecstasy
And another man is spotted in binoculars

From the sailing school   —which I survived— and the plane tree

I can no longer point out,   that stands by the harbor
                    with a hundred more,

                                        one day it was a plum tree

Or a novice nun's scream in empty fonts
                    broken by the beyond,
                                        then cooing

Of turtledoves hidden in the warm
                    gates of a stadium in the suburbs

Mientras ellas traían la pobreza,
        la señal del aborto, los cabellos,
        las manchas de salitre y,
               en las albas,

Óseo en mi rostro y largo como un tendón de aquiles
        de muchacha o de pueblo
          que camina o que duerme,

Ese olor a infinito enverjado, pujante
        junto al Crucificado
        que ocupaba,

           incorrupto,

La mitad de la balsa, del cerebro,
        de las islas del techo
          y del desagüe

—Que se arrastraba angosto, a cielo abierto,

        igual que un regimiento entre violetas,

Con hilos de agua vieja, grandes hojas
        de palmeras, tapitas de cervezas,

        campanillas silvestres, mucho tiempo
        sin Teresa, que amé a los doce años—,

While the fonts brought on poverty,
        the sign of abortion, the tresses,
        the saltpeter stains and,
                        each day at dawn,

Calcified in my face and long like the Achilles tendon
        of a girl or a people
        who walk or who sleep,

That odor of iron-gated infinity, thriving
                next to the Crucified one,
                who occupied,

                        beyond reproach,

Half of the raft, of the brain,
        of the islands on the roof
                and in the sewer

—Which slithered narrowly along, exposed,

        like a regiment marching through violets,

Its stagnant water trickling, huge fallen
        palm fronds, beer bottle caps,

        little wild bells, a long time without
        Teresa, I loved her when I was twelve—,

y la mitad

del mar:
por
donde,

me decía,

Dentro de poco el sol sería un gallo
                en un carro blindado,
                                y la cabeza

        sobre plata
        —enseguida—

        del Bautista.

and half

of the sea:
in
which,

I told myself,

The sun would soon be a rooster
                    in an armored car,
                                        and on silver

        the head
        —immediately—

        of the Baptist.

LA CASILLA DE LOS BAÑEROS, EL PISO Y EL HOMENAJE

THE BATHERS' HUT, THE FLOOR
AND THE HOMAGE

A Ernesto del Castillo,
que me prestó un salvavidas.

Vengo de comulgar y estoy en éxtasis, hermanos
           en reflejados días que tenían dos mares.

Sacristía con trigo de desnudos oyendo
           un altar de colmenas. Única sombra.
                        Tablas.

Piso para las víctimas más grises del planeta.

           Capilla sin exvotos:
           Sólo mandíbulas de escualos

Y espejito con olas que nos ve entrar cansados:

To Ernesto del Castillo,
who lent me a life jacket.

I come straight from communion and I'm in ecstasy, brothers
                on mirrored days that held two seas.

Vestry with wheat of nudes listening
                to an altar of beehives. Singular shadow.
                                Planks.

I step forth on behalf of the planet's grayest victims.

                Chapel without votives.
                Only dogfish mandibles

And a tiny mirror with waves that watch us enter exhausted:

En la gavia del tórax, como alas entre cantos
                              rodados —recogidos
                              de bruces—
                                        los pulmones;

Y, en las ceñidas lonas, ladridos empujando

                    a mástiles de hueso
                    que no fueron quebrados.

Y yo —que pude en sueños o en misión escalarme

                    por serpientes de nieve
                    que iluminan

                    escondrijos de mapas
                    y capotes

Bautizando en las noches de las cumbres a un lago—;

                    y yo —que no quisiera
                    que esa tropa oscilara

44

In the topsail of the thorax, like wings between rolled
                              songs —gathered
                              face down—
                                                  two lungs;

And, in taut sail cloths, barks pushing

              masts of bone
              that did not break.

And I —who in dreams or on a mission could climb myself

              through serpents of snow
              that illuminate

              hidden spots on maps
              and cloaks

Baptizing a lake on nights in the summits—;

              and I —who wouldn't want
              that trope to oscillate

demasiado o se hundiera
en el umbral del cielo—,

Aquí donde la novia de un buen mozo del muelle

se entregó por dinero
a las visitas

(Después de hablar los dos afuera, contra el viento,

una hora o dos horas
caminando, abrazándose)

Y a las siestas, de pie, los guardavidas

abatían la sal de sus cabezas

con una damajuana muy pesada,

De agua dulce   y de vidrio verde, grueso,

que entre todos
cuidaban,

me adormezco:

too wildly or get lost
in the threshold of the sky—,

In this place where a strapping young dock hand's bride

       sells her body
       to guests

(After the two of them speak outside, into the wind,

       and spend an hour or two
       pacing, holding each other)

And, at siesta time, the lifeguards stood up

       and rinsed the salt from their heads

       with a cumbersome demijohn

Of thick green glass, heavy with fresh water,

              that they took turns
              refilling,

                  I'm falling asleep:

Lágrima en la botella el mar se seca

Y hasta que la pequeña estufa es desatada

                           —y dejan de brillar
                             los pies oscuros—

Remolco sobre el hielo a una muchacha

(O en el piso, de nuevo,
                    veo sus pies,

                                de nuevo
                                no sé cómo

La estufa no los quema, ni sé cómo

                  no saben arder menos que ellos

                                        la cintura

O la boca,

Entreabierta en las tinieblas;

Y como siempre llueve y los relámpagos,

                  en la ventana sucia,

                                son los de ella);

A tear in a bottle the sea dries up

And until the little stove is unleashed

                                  —and her dark feet
                                    no longer gleam—

I tow a girl over the ice

(Or on the floor, again,
                     I see her feet,

                              and again
                              I don't know how

The stove doesn't scorch them, nor how

                they don't know to burn more brightly

                              than her waist

Or her mouth,

Half open in the darkness;

And it rains like always and the lightning,

                  in the dirty window,

                          is her lightning);

Y sé que lo que hicimos refulgía

                    y llamaba —ahora sé—
                    mientras lo hacíamos

Y yo no era su prójimo, ni mi yo era mi prójimo,

                    y su boca, gavilla

                    con hormigas
                    y tierra,

En confines de tinta

Me sacaba del odio.

And I know that what we did shone brightly

       and beckoned —now I know—
       while we did it

And I wasn't her neighbor, I wasn't even my own neighbor,

       and her mouth, a bundle

       of ants
       and soil,

At the ends of ink

Took me from hate.

NOTA

CRAWL fue compuesto, en alabanza a la presencia misericordiosa de Cristo Nuestro Señor, entre el 1ero. de febrero de 1980 y el 24 de junio (Natividad de San Juan Bautista) de 1982.

AUTHOR'S NOTE

CRAWL was written, praised be the merciful presence of Christ Our Lord, between February 1st, 1980 and June 24th (Nativity of St. John the Baptist), 1982.

HOSPITAL BRITÁNICO

Mi madre es la risa, la libertad, el verano.

My mother is laughter, freedom, summer.

Hospital Británico

Mes de Marzo de 1986

Pabellón Rosetto, larga esquina de verano, armadura de mariposas: Mi madre vino al cielo a visitarme.

Tengo la cabeza vendada. Permanezco en el pecho de la Luz horas y horas. Soy feliz. Me han sacado del mundo.

Mi madre es la risa, la libertad, el verano.

A veinte cuadras de aquí yace muriéndose.

Aquí besa mi paz, ve a su hijo cambiado, se prepara —en Tu llanto— para comenzar todo de nuevo.

Hospital Británico

Month of March, 1986

Rosetto Pavilion, long corner of summer, armor of butterflies: My
  mother came to heaven to visit me.

My head is bandaged. I remain in the breast of Light for hours on end.
  I am happy. They have taken me from the world.

My mother is laughter, freedom, summer.

Twenty blocks from here she lies dying.

Here she kisses my peace, sees her son changed, prepares herself —in
  Your crying— to start all over again.

Hospital Británico

Mes de Marzo de 1986

*(Versión con esquirlas
y "Christus Pantokrator")*

Pabellón Rosetto, larga esquina de verano, armadura de mariposas: Mi madre vino al cielo a visitarme.

Tengo la cabeza vendada. Permanezco en el pecho de la Luz horas y horas. Soy feliz. Me han sacado del mundo.

Mi madre es la risa, la libertad, el verano.

A veinte cuadras de aquí yace muriéndose.

Aquí besa mi paz, ve a su hijo cambiado, se prepara —en Tu llanto— para comenzar todo de nuevo.

Hospital Británico

La muchacha regresa con rostro de roedor, desfigurada por no querer saber lo que es ser joven.

Llevando otro embarazo sobre las largas piernas, me pide humildemente fechas para una lápida. (1984)

Hospital Británico

Month of March, 1986

*(Version with splinters
and "Christus Pantokrator")*

Rosetto Pavilion, long corner of summer, armor of butterflies: My
mother came to heaven to visit me.

My head is bandaged. I remain in the breast of Light for hours on end.
I am happy. They have taken me from the world.

My mother is laughter, freedom, summer.

Twenty blocks from here she lies dying.

Here she kisses my peace, sees her son changed, prepares herself —in
Your crying— to start all over again.

Hospital Británico

The girl returns with the face of a rodent, disfigured by not wanting to
know what it means to be young.

Carrying another pregnancy on her long legs, she meekly asks me to
give her dates for a tombstone. (1984)

Hospital Británico

¿Quién puso en mí esa misa a la que nunca llego? ¿Quién puso en mi camino hacia la misa a esos patos marrones —o pupitres con las alas abiertas— que se hunden en el polvo de la tarde sobre la pérgola que cubrían las glicinas? (1984)

Hospital Británico

Voy hacia lo que menos conocí en mi vida: voy hacia mi cuerpo. (1984)

Pabellón Rosetto

Aquella blanca pared nueva, joven, que hablaba a las palmeras de una playa —enfermeras de pechos de luz verde— en una fotografía que perdí en mi adolescencia.

Pabellón Rosetto

Soñé que nos hundíamos y que después nadábamos hacia la costa lentamente y que de nuestras sombras de color verde claro huían los tiburones. (1978)

Pabellón Rosetto

Si me enseñaras qué es el verde claro... (1978)

Hospital Británico

Who placed in me that mass I never reach? Who littered my way to mass with those brown ducks —or writing desks with spread wings— that sink into the dust of afternoon above the wisteria-covered arbor? (1984)

Hospital Británico

I go toward the thing I knew least in my life: I go toward my body. (1984)

Rosetto Pavilion

That white wall, fresh and young, that spoke to the palms on a beach —nurses with breasts of green light— in a photograph I lost in my adolescence.

Rosetto Pavilion

I dreamed we were sinking and then we were swimming languidly toward the shore and the sharks fled from our light green shadows. (1978)

Rosetto Pavilion

If only you would show me what light green is... (1978)

Pabellón Rosetto

Es difícil llegar a la capilla: se puede orar entre las cañas en el viento debajo de la cama. (1984)

"Christus Pantokrator"

La postal tiene una leyenda: "Christus Pantokrator, siglo XIII."

A los pies de la pared desnuda, la postal es un Christus Pantokrator en la mitad de un espigón larguísimo. (1985)

"Christus Pantokrator"

Entre mis ojos y los ojos de Christus Pantokrator nunca hay piso. Siempre hay dos alpargatas descosidas, blancas, en un día de viento.

Con la postal en el zócalo, con Christus Pantokrator en el espigón larguísimo, mi oscuridad no tiene hambre de gaviotas. (1985)

"Christus Pantokrator"

La postal viene de marineros, de pugilistas viejos en ese bar estrecho que parece un submarino —de maderas y latas— hundiéndose en el sol de la ribera.

La postal viene de un Christus Pantokrator que cuando bajo las persianas, apago la luz y cierro los ojos, me pide que filme Su Silencio dentro de una botella varada en un banco infinito. (1985)

Rosetto Pavilion

The chapel is hard to find: one can pray among the reeds in the wind beneath one's bed. (1984)

"Christus Pantokrator"

The postcard has a caption: "Christus Pantokrator, 13th Century."

At the foot of the bare wall, the postcard is a Christus Pantokrator halfway to the end of a very long jetty. (1985)

"Christus Pantokrator"

Between my eyes and the eyes of Christus Pantokrator there is never a floor. There is always a pair of white espadrilles on a windy day, coming undone.

With the postcard on the baseboard, with Christus Pantokrator on the very long jetty, my darkness has no hunger for seagulls. (1985)

"Christus Pantokrator"

The postcard comes from sailors, from old pugilists in that narrow bar like a submarine —of tin cans and wood— sinking into the coastal sun.

The postcard comes from a Christus Pantokrator, who, when I lower the blinds, turn off the light, and close my eyes, asks me to film His Silence in a bottle washed up on an endless shoal. (1985)

"Christus Pantokrator"

Delante de la postal estoy como una pala que cava en el sol, en el Rostro y en los ojos de Christus Pantokrator. (1985)

Sé que sólo en los ojos de Christus Pantokrator puedo cavar en la transpiración de todos mis veranos hasta llegar desde el esternón, desde el mediodía, a ese faro cubierto por alas de naranjos que quiero para el niño casi mudo que llevé sobre el alma muchos meses. (Mes de Abril de 1986)

Larga esquina de verano

Alguien me odió ante el sol al que mi madre me arrojó. Necesito estar a oscuras, necesito regresar al hombre. No quiero que me toque la muchacha, ni el rufián, ni el ojo del poder, ni la ciencia del mundo. No quiero ser tocado por los sueños.

El enano que es mi ángel de la guarda sube bamboleándose los pocos peldaños de madera ametrallados por los soles; y sobre el pasamano de coronas de espinas, la piedra de su anillo es un cruzado que trepa somnoliento una colina: burdeles vacíos y pequeños, panaderías abiertas pero muy pequeñas, teatros pequeños pero cerrados —y más arriba ojos de catacumbas, lejanas miradas de catacumbas tras oscuras pestañas a flor de tierra.

Un tiburón se pudre a veinte metros. Un tiburón pequeño —una bala con tajos, un acordeón abierto —se pudre y me acompaña. Un tiburón —un criquet en silencio en el suelo de tierra, junto a un tambor de agua, en una gomería a muchos metros de la ruta— se pudre a veinte metros del sol en mi cabeza: El sol como las puertas,

"Christus Pantokrator"

In front of the postcard I am like a shovel that digs in the sun, in the Face and in the eyes of Christus Pantokrator. (1985)

I know that only in the eyes of Christus Pantokrator can I dig in the perspiration of all my summers until I arrive from my sternum, from noon, at that lighthouse shaded by the limbs of orange trees that I want for the half-mute boy I bore for many months upon my soul. (Month of April, 1986)

Long corner of summer

Someone hated me before the sun into which I was cast by my mother. I need to be in the dark, I need to return to man. I don't want the girl to touch me, nor the pimp, nor the eye of power, nor worldly science. I don't want to be touched by dreams.

The dwarf who is my guardian angel sways back and forth as he comes up the few wooden steps riddled with suns; and along the banister of thorny crowns, the stone in his ring is a crusader climbing a hill in a daze: small, deserted brothels, bakeries that are open but very small, theaters that are small but closed —and above them the eyes of catacombs, distant gazes of catacombs behind dark eyelashes at ground level.

A shark rots twenty meters from here. A small shark —a bullet with slits, an open accordion— rots and is my companion. A shark rots —a fishing reel silent on the dirt floor, next to a water drum, in a tire shop set back from the highway— twenty meters from the sun in my head: The sun like the doors, flanked by two men in pure

con dos hombres blanquísimos, de un colegio militar en un desierto; un colegio militar que no es más que un desierto en un lugar adentro de esta playa de la que huye el futuro. (1984)

Larga esquina de verano

¿Nunca morirá la sensación de que el demonio puede servirse de los cielos, y de las nubes y las aves, para observarme las entrañas?

Amigos muertos que caminan en las tardes grises hacia frontones de pelota solitarios: El rufián que me mira se sonríe como si yo pudiera desearla todavía.

Se nubla y se desnubla. Mu hundo en mi carne; me hundo en la iglesia de desagüe a cielo abierto en la que creo. Espero la resurrección —espero su estallido contra mis enemigos— en este cuerpo, en este día, en esta playa. Nada puede impedir que en su Pierna me azoten como cota de malla —y sin ninguna Historia ardan en mí— las cabezas de fósforos de todo el Tiempo.

Tengo las toses de los viejos fusiles de un Tiro Federal en los ojos. Mi vida es un desierto entre dos guerras. Necesito estar a oscuras. Necesito dormir, pero el sol me despierta. El sol, a través de mis párpados, como alas de gaviotas que echan cal sobre toda mi vida; el sol como una zona que me había olvidado; el sol como un golpe de espuma en mis confines; el sol como dos jóvenes vigías en una tempestad de luz que se ha tragado al mar, a las velas y al cielo. (1984)

Larga esquina de verano

La boca abierta al viento que se lleva a las moscas, el tiburón se pudre a veinte metros. El tiburón se desvanece, flota sobre el último asiento

white, of a military school in the desert; a military school that is no more than a desert in a place inside this beach from which the future flees. (1984)

Long corner of summer

Will it never end, this feeling that the devil can take what he wants from the heavens, from the clouds and birds, just to get a look at my guts?

Dead friends who walk toward deserted handball courts on grey afternoons: The pimp watching me smiles as if I were still able to desire his girl.

It gets cloudy and it unclouds. I sink into my flesh; I sink into that open sewer of a church in which I believe. I wait for the resurrection —I wait for it to shatter my enemies— in this body, on this day, on this beach. Nothing can stop the match heads of Time in its entirety — and without any History they burn inside me— from lashing me like chain mail as I lay across his Leg.

I have the coughs of old rifles at a Federal Range in my eyes. My life is a desert between two wars. I need to be in the dark. I need to sleep, but the sun wakes me. The sun, through my eyelids, like the wings of gulls that scatter whitewash across my whole life; the sun like a place that had forgotten me; the sun like pounding surf against my limits; the sun like two young watchmen in a tempest of light that has swallowed the sea, the sails and the sky. (1984)

Long corner of summer

Its mouth open to the breeze that carries away the flies, the shark rots twenty meters from here. The shark vanishes, it floats over the last

de la playa —del ómnibus que asciende con las ratas mareadas y
con frío y comienza a partirse por la mitad y a desprenderse del
limpiaparabrisas, que en los ojos del mar era su lluvia.

Me acostumbré a verlas llegar con las nubes para cambiar mi vida. Me
acostumbré a extrañarlas bajo el cielo: calladas, sin equipaje, con un
cepillo de dientes entre sus manos. Me acostumbré a sus vientres
sin esposo, embarazadas jóvenes que odian la arena que me cubre.
(1984)

Larga esquina de verano

¿Toda la arena de esta playa quiere llenar mi boca? Ya todo hambre de
Rostro ensangrentado quiere comer arena y olvidarse?

Aves marinas que regresan de la velocidad de Dios en mi cabeza: No me
separo de las claras paralelas de madera que tatuaban la piel de mis
brazos junto a las axilas; no me separo de la única morada —sin
paredes ni techo— que he tenido en el ígneo brillante de extranjero
del centro de los patios vacíos del verano, y soy hambre de arenas
—y hambre de Rostro ensangrentado.

Pero como sitiado por una eternidad, ¿yo puedo hacer violencia
para que aparezca Tu Cuerpo, que es mi arrepentimiento? ¿Puedo
hacer violencia con el pugilista africano de hierro y vientre
almohadillado que es mi pieza sin luz a la una de la tarde mientras
el mar —afuera— parece una armería? Dos mil años de esperanza,
de arena y de muchacha muerta, ¿pueden hacer violencia? Con
humedad de tienda que vendía cigarrillos negros, revólveres baratos
y cintas de colores para disfraces de Carnaval, ¿se puede todavía
hacer violencia?

seat on the beach —on the bus that rises with cold, seasick rats and starts to split down the middle and separate from its windshield wipers, which in the eyes of the sea were its rain.

I got used to watching them show up with the clouds to change my life. I got used to pining for them under the firmament: silent, without luggage, their toothbrushes in their hands. I got used to their bellies without husbands, these pregnant girls who hate the sand piled over me. (1984)

Long corner of summer

Does all the sand on this beach hope to fill my mouth? And does all hunger for blood-stained Face hope to feast on sand and be forgotten?

Marine birds that come back from the velocity of God in my head: I don't separate myself from the clear wooden parallels that tattooed the skin of my biceps near my armpits; I don't separate myself from the only home I've ever known —it has neither walls nor roof— perched on volcanic rock of foreign brilliance in the center of deserted summer patios, and I am hunger for sands —and hunger for blood-stained Face.

But as one besieged by an eternity, can I commit an act of violence that would conjure Your Body, which is my repentance? Can I commit an act of violence alongside the ironclad African pugilist with the padded belly who is my room without light at one in the afternoon while the sea   outside— seems like an armory? Can two thousand years of hope, of sand and of dead girl, commit an act of violence? In air as damp as a store that sold black cigarettes, cheap revolvers, and colorful ribbons for costumes worn at Carnaval, even then can one commit an act of violence?

Sin Tu Cuerpo en la tierra muere sin sangre el que no muere mártir; sin Tu Cuerpo en la tierra soy la trastienda de un negocio donde se deshacen cadenas, brújulas, timones —lentamente como hostias— bajo un ventilador de techo gris; sin Tu Cuerpo en la tierra no sé cómo pedir perdón a una muchacha en la punta de guadaña con rocío del ala izquierda del cementerio alemán (y la orilla del mar —espuma y agua helada en las mejillas— es a veces un hombre que se afeita sin ganas día tras día). (1985)

Larga esquina de verano

¿Soy ese tripulante con corona de espinas que no ve a sus alas afuera del buque, que no ve a Tu Rostro en el afiche pegado al casco y desgarrado por el viento y que no sabe todavía que Tu Rostro es más que todo el mar cuando lanza sus dados contra un negro espigón de cocinas de hierro que espera a algunos hombres en un sol donde nieva? (1985)

Tu Rostro

Tu Rostro como sangre muy oscura en un plato de tropa, entre cocinas frías y bajo un sol de nieve; Tu Rostro como una conversación entre colmenas con vértigo en la llanura del verano; Tu Rostro como sombra verde y negra con balidos muy cerca de mi aliento y mi revólver; Tu Rostro como sombra verde y negra que desciende al galope, cada tarde, desde una pampa a dos mil metros sobre el nivel del mar; Tu Rostro como arroyos de violetas cayendo lentamente desde gallos de riña; Tu Rostro como arroyos de violetas que empapan de vitrales a un hospital sobre un barranco. (1985)

Without Your Body on earth the man who doesn't die a martyr dies bloodless; without Your Body on earth I am the back room of a shop where chains, compasses, rudders are taken apart —carefully, like hosts— beneath a fan attached to a grey ceiling; without Your Body on earth I don't know how to beg for forgiveness from a girl on the end of a scythe covered in dew from the left wing of the German cemetery (and sometimes the shoreline —foam and frozen water on its cheeks— is a man who begrudgingly shaves day after day). (1985)

Long corner of summer

Am I that crew member with a crown of thorns who can't see his wings outside the ship, who can't see Your Face in the poster nailed to the hull and torn by the wind and who still doesn't know that Your Face is greater than the entire sea when it throws its dice against a black jetty of iron stoves that waits for some men in a sun where it snows? (1985)

Your Face

Your Face like darkest blood on a soldier's plate, among cold stoves and beneath a snowy sun; Your Face like a conversation between frenzied hives on summer's plain; Your Face like green and black shadow with bleating so close to my breath and my revolver; Your Face like green and black shadow that comes down at a gallop, each afternoon, from a pampa two thousand meters above sea level; Your Face like streams of violets slowly falling from cocks bred to fight; Your Face like streams of violets that bathe a hospital in stained glass above a ravine. (1985)

Tu Cuerpo y Tu Padre

Tu Cuerpo como un barranco, y el amor de Tu Padre como duras mazorcas de tristeza en Tus axilas casi desgarradas. (1985)

Tengo la cabeza vendada (texto profético lejano)

Mi cabeza para nacer cruza el fuego del mundo pero con una serpentina de agua helada en la memoria. Y le pido socorro. (1978)

Tengo la cabeza vendada

Mariposa de Dios, pubis de María: Atraviesa la sangre de mi frente —**hasta besarme el Rostro en Jesucristo (1982)**—.

Tengo la cabeza vendada (textos proféticos)

Mi cuerpo —con aves bisturíes en la frente— entra en mi alma. (1984)

El sol, en mi cabeza, como toda la sangre de Cristo sobre una pared de anestesia total. (1984)

Santa Reina de los misterios del rosario del hacha y de las brazadas lejos del espigón: Ruega por mí que estoy en una zona donde nunca había anclado con maniobras de Cristo en mi cabeza. (1985)

Señor: Desde este instante mi cabeza quiere ser, por los siglos de los siglos, la herida de Tu Mano bendiciéndome en fuego. (1984)

Your Body and Your Father

Your body like a ravine, and Your Father's love like hard cobs of sadness in Your armpits about to tear apart. (1985)

My head is bandaged (distant prophetic text)

My head passes through the fire of the world to be born but keeps a winding stream of frozen water in its memory. And I ask it to help me. (1978)

My head is bandaged

Butterfly of God, pubis of Mary: Cross the blood of my brow —**until I kiss my very Face in Jesus Christ** (1982)—.

My head is bandaged (prophetic texts)

My body —with scalpel birds on its brow— enters my soul. (1984)

The sun, in my head, like all the blood of Christ against a wall of total anesthesia. (1984)

Holy Queen of the mysteries of the rosary of the axe and of strokes far from the jetty: Pray for me who am in a place where I had never anchored with maneuvers of Christ in my head. (1985)

Lord: From this moment on my head wishes to be, for centuries upon centuries, the wound on Your Hand as you bless me in fire. (1984)

El sol como la blanca velocidad de Dios en mi cabeza, que la aspira y desgarra hacia la nuca. (1984)

Tengo la cabeza vendada (texto del hombre en la playa)

El sol entra con mi alma en mi cabeza (o mi cuerpo —con la Resurrección— entra en mi alma). (1984)

Tengo la cabeza vendada (texto del hombre en la playa)

Por culpa del viento de fuego que penetra en su herida, en este instante, Tu Mano traza un ancla y no una cruz en mi cabeza.

Quiero beber hacia mi nuca, eternamente, los dos brazos del ancla del temblor de Tu Carne y de la prisa de los Cielos. (1984)

Tengo la cabeza vendada (texto del hombre en la playa)

Allá atrás, en mi nuca, vi al blanquísimo desierto de esta vida de mi vida; vi a mi eternidad, que debo atravesar desde los ojos del Señor hasta los ojos del Señor. (1984)

Me han sacado del mundo

Soy el lugar donde el Señor tiende la Luz que Él es.

The sun like the white velocity of God in my head, which it breathes in and tears to the nape. (1984)

My head is bandaged (text by the man on the beach)

Along with my soul the sun enters into my head (or my body —along with the Resurrection— enters into my soul). (1984)

My head is bandaged (text by the man on the beach)

It is the fault of the fiery wind that pierces its wound, at this moment, that Your Hand traces an anchor in my head and not a cross.

I want to drink back to my nape, forever, the two arms of the anchor of the trembling of Your Flesh and of the Heavens' haste. (1984)

My head is bandaged (text by the man on the beach)

Back there, on my nape, I saw the pure white desert of this life of my life; I saw my eternity, which I must traverse from the eyes of the Lord to the eyes of the Lord. (1984)

They have taken me from the world

I am the place where the Lord spreads out the Light that He is.

Me han sacado del mundo

Me cubre una armadura de mariposas y estoy en la camisa de mariposas que es el Señor —adentro, en mí.

El Reino de los Cielos me rodea. El Reino de los Cielos es el Cuerpo de Cristo —y cada mediodía toco a Cristo.

Cristo es Cristo madre, y en Él viene mi madre a visitarme.

Me han sacado del mundo

"Mujer que embaracé," "Pabellón Rosetto," "Larga esquina de verano":

Vuelve el placer de las palabras a mi carne en las copas de unos eucaliptus (o en los altos de "B," desde los cuales una vez —sólo una vez— vi a una playa del cielo recostada en la costa).

Me han sacado del mundo

Manos de María, sienes de mármol de mi playa en el cielo:

La muerte es el comienzo de una guerra donde jamás otro hombre podrá ver mi esqueleto.

La libertad, el verano (A mi madre, recordándole el fuego)

Porque parto recién cuando he sudado y abro una canilla y me acuclillo como junto a un altar, como escondido, y el chorro cae

They have taken me from the world

An armor of butterflies covers me and I wear the shirt of butterflies
that is the Lord —within, inside me.

The Kingdom of Heaven surrounds me. The Kingdom of Heaven is
the Body of Christ —and each day at noon I touch Christ.

Christ is Christ the mother, and my mother comes to visit me in Him.

They have taken me from the world

"Woman I impregnated," "Rosetto Pavilion," "Long corner of summer":

The pleasure of words comes back to my flesh in the tops of some
eucalyptus trees (or in the heights of "B," where once   just once— I
looked out and saw a heavenly beach leaning against the shore).

They have taken me from the world

Hands of Mary, temples of marble from my beach in heaven:

Death is the beginning of a war in which another man will never be
able to see my skeleton.

Freedom, summer (To my mother, reminding her of the fire)

Because I depart just when I've begun to sweat and I turn on the faucet
and lower myself as if I were beside an altar, as if I were hiding, and

helado en mi cabeza y desliza su hostia hacia mis labios, envuelta en los cabellos que la siguen. (1976)

Vengo de comulgar y estoy en éxtasis aunque comulgué con los cosacos sentados a una mesa bajo el cielo y los eucaliptus que con ellos se cimbran estos días bochornosos en que camino hasta las areneras del sur de la ciudad —el vizcaíno, santa adela, la elisa. (1982)

Por las paredes de los rascacielos el calor y el silencio suben de nave en nave: Obsesivo verano de fotógrafo en fotógrafo, ojos del Arponero que rayan lo que miran. Ser de avenidas verticales que jamás fue azotado. (1978)

Después íbamos al África cada día de nuevo —antes que nada, antes de vestirnos— mientras rugían las fieras abajo en el zoológico, subía un sol sangriento a sus jazmines, y nosotros nos odiábamos, nos deseábamos, gritábamos... (1978)

Instantes de anestesia, de lento alcohol de anoche todavía en la sangre de pie de una muchacha desnuda y más dorada que la escoba: Necesito aferrarme de nuevo a la llanura, al ave blanca del corpiño en la pileta de lavar, detrás de la estación y entre las casuarinas. (1984)

Tengo la foto de dos novios que cayeron al mar. Están vestidos de invierno, los invito a desnudarse. En las siestas nos sentamos junto a la bomba de agua y nos miramos: de nuevo embolsan luz los pechos de ella: él amaba a los caballos y una vez intentó suicidarse. (1978)

Necesito oler limón, necesito oler limón. De tanto respirar este aire azul, este cielo encarnizadamente azul, se pueden reventar los vasos de sangre más pequeños de mi nariz. (1969)

80

the freezing water falls on my head and slides its host toward my
lips, wrapped in the tresses that come after it. (1976)

I come straight from communion and I'm in ecstasy though I took it
with the Cossacks seated at a table beneath the sky and the
eucalyptus trees that sway alongside them these muggy days when
I walk to the sand quarries south of the city —el vizcaíno, santa
adela, la elisa. (1982)

Heat and silence climb the walls of the skyscrapers from nave to nave:
Obsessive summer from photographer to photographer, eyes of the
Harpooner that stripe what they see. Being of vertical avenues that's
never been lashed. (1978)

Then we went to Africa every day as if for the first time —before anything
else, before we got dressed— while the beasts roared below us in the
preserve, a bleeding sun rose before its jasmines, and we hated each
other, we desired each other, we were screaming... (1978)

Moments of anesthesia, of last night's alcohol lingering in the blood
taken from the foot of a naked girl more golden than a broom. Again
I need to cling to smoothness, to that white bird of a bra in the
washtub, behind the station and among the casuarinas. (1984)

I hold the photo of two lovers who fell into the sea. They're dressed for
winter, I ask them to take off their clothes. During siestas we sit beside
the water pump and stare at each other: light collects in her breasts
again; he loved horses and one time he tried to kill himself. (1978)

I need to smell lemon, I need to smell lemon. The tiniest blood vessels
in my nose could burst from breathing in so much of this blue air,
this sky so viciously blue. (1969)

Y a las siestas, de pie, los guardavidas abatían la sal de sus cabezas
con una damajuana muy pesada, de agua dulce y de vidrio verde,
grueso, que entre todos cuidaban. (1982)

Yace muriéndose

Toda la transpiración de mi cuerpo regresará a mis ojos cuando muera
el tambor en donde fui formado y hablé con Él —como un niño
borracho— entre sillas caídas, río crecido y juncos.

Todas las lágrimas de mi vida volverán a mis ojos; y por las hondas sedas
de un pecho de caballo querré internarme, huir, refugiarme en mi
casa de trozos esparcidos de ballenas: mi casa como cuerpo de varón
recién nacido en el tórrido vientre del silencio. (1985)

Yace muriéndose

Nunca más pasaré junto al bar que daba al patio de la Capitanía. No
miraré la mesa donde fuimos felices:

El sol como ese lugar bajo las aguas de un río de tierra y de naranjas donde
antes de aprender a caminar miré a Dios como un hombre que sabe
qué es la guerra. El sol como esas aguas de tierra y de naranjas donde
sin extrañar la respiración, el aire, lo miré de este modo: "Recuerdo una
victoria lejana (tantos salvados rostros que **después** nadie quiere
recordarme) y estoy en paz con mi conciencia todavía." (1984)

Yace muriéndose

La dejé sobre un lecho de vincapervincas altas, frías, violáceas.

And, at siesta time, the lifeguards stood up and rinsed the salt from their heads with a cumbersome demijohn of thick green glass, heavy with fresh water, that they took turns refilling. (1982)

She lies dying

All my body's perspiration will return to my eyes when the drum in which I was created and spoke to Him —like a drunk boy— dies among toppled chairs, cresting river and reeds.

All my life's tears will return to my eyes; and I'll want to bury myself in the deep silks of a horse's chest, to flee, to hide in my house of scattered whale parts: my house like the body of a boy recently born into the torrid belly of silence. (1985)

She lies dying

I'll never again walk past the bar that faced the Headquarters' patio. I won't look upon the table where we were happy:

The sun like that place beneath the waters of a river of soil and oranges where before learning to walk I looked upon God as a man who knows what war is. The sun like those waters of soil and oranges where without yearning for breath, for air, I looked upon him in this way: "I remember a far-off victory (so many saved faces that **afterwards** nobody wants to remember me) and I'm at peace with my conscience to this day." (1984)

She lies dying

I left her on a deathbed of tall, cold, purplish periwinkles.

Por su final de arroyo, la herida de mi frente llora en las flores y agradece.

Yace muriéndose

Dentro de cuatro días llegará a Tu Océano con uno de mis soldaditos dormido sobre sus labios. Y se dirá, sonriéndome: "Es lo poco que hace que este hombre iba al centro del sol cada mañana con un puñado de soldados de plomo. Es lo poco que hace que en el centro del sol, cada mañana, su corazón era un puñado de soldados de plomo entre gallos."

Dormido sobre sus labios

Pequeño legionario, ¡cuánto viento! Pedacito de plomo, pedacito de Sahara: Vendrán veranos no obsesivos; pasarán los hijos de mis hijos. (1978)

Yo puedo hachar todo el día pero no puedo cavar todo el día. No puedo cavar en ningún lado sin estar esperando que aparezca de pronto un soldado de plomo entre mis pies desnudos. (1978)

Para comenzar todo de nuevo

Es mi parte de tierra la que llora por los ciruelos que ha perdido.

Para comenzar todo de nuevo

El verano en que resucitemos tendrá un molino cerca con un chorro blanquísimo sepultado en la vena. (1969)

For its stream-like finale, the wound on my forehead cries in the flowers and gives thanks.

She lies dying

Within four days she'll reach Your Ocean with one of my little toy soldiers asleep upon her lips. And smiling at me, she'll say to herself: "It wasn't long ago that this man went to the center of the sun each morning with a handful of tin soldiers. It wasn't long ago that in the center of the sun, each morning, his heart was a handful of tin soldiers among roosters."

Asleep upon her lips

How windy it is, little legionnaire! Tiny piece of tin, tiny piece of Sahara: There will be summers free of obsession; the sons of my sons shall pass. (1978)

I can chop all day but I can't dig all day. I can't dig anywhere without fully expecting a tin soldier to appear suddenly between my naked feet. (1978)

To start all over again

My piece of earth is the one that cries for the plum trees it has lost.

To start all over again

The summer we rise from the dead will have a mill nearby with a jet-white stream buried in its vein. (1969)

85

NOTA

Corresponden al mes de marzo de 1986 los únicos textos de HOSPITAL BRITÁNICO *que no van acompañados por su fecha de redacción. Los pertenecientes a los años 1985 y 1984 ven la luz por primera vez en este libro, mientras los de 1982, 1978, 1976 y 1969 fueron ya publicados por el autor en* CRAWL, LEGIÓN EXTRANJERA, CARTA DE MAREAR *y* HUMANAE VITAE MIA.

AUTHOR'S NOTE

The texts in HOSPITAL BRITÁNICO that are not accompanied by dates correspond to the month of March, 1986. Those that were written during the years 1984 and 1985 see light of day for the first time in this book, while those from 1982, 1978, 1976 and 1969 were previously published by the author in CRAWL, FOREIGN LEGION, NAUTICAL CHART and HUMANAE VITAE MIA.

VIEL TEMPERLEY: STATE OF COMMUNION

This interview, conducted by Sergio Bizzio, originally appeared in Revista Vuelta Sudamericana, *No. 12, July, 1987, Buenos Aires.*

Viel Temperley was born in Buenos Aires in 1933. At just 23, his first book won the Medal of Honor from the Society of Argentine Writers. Thirty years have flown by since the appearance of that book and his most recent one. His few readers speak of Viel as one of the best contemporary writers. He's just arrived from a radiation treatment and is lying in bed, a blanket tidily folded over his chest.

—Watch out—he signals, smiling, and the phone in the room starts to ring.

Throughout the room are pictures painted by Viel or by Luisa, his girlfriend. There's a tall, well-built bookcase surrounded by photographs and a blue Christ hemmed in by a grove of flowerless plants. Viel is not a poet of Mallarmé-like whispering. He doesn't speak of "a text, finally real, that will serve as the Orphic explication of Earth," nor of "a Cosmos organized under the sign of beauty." He says: "my work had to be a complete world." (A while ago, thumbing through the novel of a genius, intimidated by the reverberations of his success, it occurred to me that the perception of beauty has more to do with sensations than with judgment —a facile a facile thought, but its anachronism is appealing. Isn't there a god who automatically disappears if he's called upon too often?) And if he talks about his books —in this case *Foreign Legion* (1978), *Crawl* (1982), and *Hospital Británico* (1986)— he does exactly the opposite of those persons who, as Arreola would say, fall into each others' arms without giving any details about their affair.

—Unplug it— he orders. I don't want anyone to interrupt me.

I mention to him that it seems as if he had appeared on the scene quite suddenly this past year, when he already had put out nine books.

—I think that's my own fault. I didn't do anything to make myself better known. I wasn't a member of any group. I always recoiled from book parties. And when *Nautical Chart* came out, in 1976, I had already published five books... but it was my intention to cause a rupture in my poetry; I found it too rigid, like it was stuck to a mold, a beginning, middle, and end: I knew what I was going to say. Then I went on to say it, to see it. What began to interest me was poetry that allowed me not only to conceal myself but to avoid myself and to create a world, to hold a world.

—What were you trying to avoid?

—Things that were too clear. I would destroy myself in each image in order to conceal myself, but I would leave behind (in *Foreign Legion*, for instance) dates and characters that made disparate poems into a single poem. So afterwards, when I had the opportunity to just forget about everything, I shut myself in with a title, *Crawl*, and the intention to give testimony of my faith in Christ, whom I had never named before: I said "God"; a pantheistic god, not the son, the man. And the fact is I found myself in my poetry when I no longer knew how to write it. I ended up explaining how to swim, how to position the hands when swimming...

But I discovered that in order to write *Crawl* I had to learn to pray, and I began to have a distinctly new relationship to prayer and the breath. And at the end of the day I found that I was mentioning him as "this man" or "that man," with lower case letters, because in that moment of my spiritual life it would have been a lie to repeatedly put down "Jesus Christ." Throughout the entire book I only call him by name a single time. I had no right to use that name.

—More than the search for The Name, this seems like the search for a name. Or do you consider yourself a religious poet?

—A religious poet? No. Not at all. I might be a mystic, a surrealist poet, whatever you want, but not religious. I write about sailors and swimmers. Jesus Christ appears in the form of a pimp, a vagrant, a bather. I wrote "Kiss my very face in Jesus Christ" because I wanted to say that Christ had allowed me to kiss myself through him. Kissing myself, but through him, that's what interests me. I don't orient myself towards him by putting aside my love for the girl lying next to the lamp: I look for him there. It was enough for me to have written his name a single time. I gave testimony. Big deal. Afterwards I busied myself with the cover, with the sailor from a John Player cigarette box... I used to believe that he really existed. An uncle had introduced him to me in a room covered in floral wallpaper. And I remember that I loved him. But I never saw him again until much later, on a pack of cigarettes. I had dreamed about him, and I assumed his was the face of Christ. God looks just like a sailor, a Jewish sailor perhaps, with a strong, square jaw. Anyway, in place of a life jacket, I asked a friend to draw a crown of thorns. Finally, it occurred to me to add the formatting. If you look at *Crawl* from above it moves like a swimming body. I spread the poem out on the floor and stood on a chair to see if there were things that exceeded the pattern. I spent hours above that chair smoking and looking, and making corrections so that it would have that form. I even tried to make sure that the stanzas didn't have any periods until the last part, because I wanted it to be like breathing, I wanted each stroke to represent a breath. Only at the end, when it talks about other men, are there periods and interruptions. But where it's pure swimming, there are only stanzas.

—And with respect to the leitmotif, "I come straight from communion and I'm in ecstasy?"

—That happened one day when I was terribly anxious and went into the Santísimo, the church that's over here behind the Kavanagh. For whatever reason I couldn't bear to be inside. I left, I sat down on the lawn, in the plaza, and I immediately had a sensation of extraordinary ecstasy... And I told myself that that was the motif that should begin each part. And in the first part it continues "though I took it like a drowned man." That part, like a drowned man... Another time, I was walking through the port, and in the middle of a row of plane trees I felt an attack of God, I was struck by God, and I began to cry. There's a plane tree in *Crawl*. I also remember how when I was very young and living in Vicente López, every morning my mother would carry me on her back down to the river. This was before I could walk. And one day I fell into the water. I remember that I was sitting under the water in peace, and didn't miss life, or breathing, or the world, at all. The only thing I felt was ecstasy when I saw an earth-colored wall lit up by the sun: there was an orange veil before my eyes. And I was happy.

—In *The Swimmer* you write of "...water so blue that the man / entered into it and breathed."

—He breathes the sky. That's why *Crawl* was enough for me until I closed my eyes on the beach one cloudy day and saw two incredibly white figures, and I told myself that I was going to write about those two guys standing guard in the sand. That book would become *Hospital Británico*. I was in the Británico. I became sick when I saw my mother waiting to die, and she did die four days after they drilled a hole in my skull. The two of us had spent three months lying in bed. Anyway, they operate on my head and two or three days later I go out into the garden. I was on my girlfriend's arm. We sat down behind a pavilion, the one I call the Rosetto Pavilion. Butterflies were flying around and there were these very beautiful eucalyptus trees, nothing more than that, and I was surrounded and pierced by a feeling of love so intense that it ruined worldly life for me.

—How?

—Yes, the feeling of being surrounded by sky, and of that sky touching me like flesh, and I could be the flesh of Christ and at the same time I had Christ inside of me... I was loved with an intensity that was almost unbearable. That lasted one week. When I went home I laid down in the living room and opened the window so that the breeze could move the ivy covering it and I was up until dawn trying to recover that state of communion, but nothing happened.

—Well, *Hospital Británico* happened.

—A book by a man with a hole in his head. The man who wrote that poem doesn't exist anymore. At that time (I didn't know they were going to give me radiation), I ran out the door flying; I was going to write. The splinters occurred to me as a solution, I gave it an order, I wrote the parts about my mother's death... and the rest was done by a guy who was in a state of having left reality because he had an egg in his head. Afterwards, yes, afterwards they had to give me radiation. Who the hell put that thing together? I have no idea. People come by, people visit me, letters arrive, but I have very little to do with the overall effect of that book. I'm not the author of *Hospital Británico* like I was the author of *Crawl*. *Hospital Británico* is something that was in the air. I did nothing more than find it. *Hospital Británico* allows me to believe that I left the world and I don't know what for. Heaven was in the nurse passing by....

ACKNOWLEDGMENTS

There are several people whose assistance and close readings of these translations have been indispensable. Melanie Nicholson helped me develop the earliest drafts, and editor Arlo Haskell's guidance and attention to nuances in the text shaped the final ones. In Buenos Aires, Francisco Garamona and Cecilia Pavón answered innumerable questions regarding interpretation and context; our subsequent online chats and rapid-fire email volleys make me wonder how translation was done before the advent of the internet. Sergio Bizzio's interview brings an added dimension to the portrait of Viel Temperley that comes through in the poetry. Carlos Pereiro from Ediciones del Dock, Viel Temperley's Argentine publisher, played an important role in making this project happen. And I am most grateful for Brigid McCaffrey's company on all journeys, actual and spiritual, related to its realization.

My profound appreciation goes to Héctor Viel Temperley's family, especially his son Juan Viel Temperley, who was my first point of contact, and his daughter Soledad Viel Temperley, whose encouragement and collaboration allowed me to carry on the legacy of their father's work.

S.K.

TRANSLATOR'S NOTE

The source for the Spanish text of *Crawl* is Héctor Viel Temperley's original 1982 edition, published by Par-Avi-Cygno. The sources for *Hospital Británico* are the 1997 second edition and the 2003 *Complete Works*, both published by Ediciones del Dock.

The source texts include several instances of unorthodox capitalization. These are reproduced in the Spanish text here, and are reflected in the English. Every effort has been made to maintain the unique shape of *Crawl* as it was first published.

An epigraph for *Crawl,* cited as Psalm 89,26, is from the Spanish version of the Jerusalem Bible. In its English version, this appears as Psalm 89,25. I have allowed the discrepancy to stand. However, I have included the English translation of the verse from the New International Version, as it is closer to the spirit of the text chosen by Viel Temperley.

On its back cover the original edition of *Crawl* featured the following Biblical citation (in Spanish), identified as Matthew 12,3:

> Have you not read what David did when he was hungry, and they that were with him, how he entered into the house of God and did eat the bread of the Presence, which it was not lawful for him to eat, nor for them that were with him, but for the priests only?